MAKING A BETTER WRLD

# Protecting Our Air, Land, and Water

## By Gary Chandler and Kevin Graham

Twenty-First Century Books

A Division of Henry Holt and Company
New York

Twenty-First Century Books
A division of Henry Holt and Company, Inc.
115 West 18th Street
New York, New York 10011

Henry Holt® and colophon are registered trademarks of
Henry Holt and Company, Inc.
*Publishers since 1866*

Published in Canada by Fitzhenry & Whiteside Ltd.
195 Allstate Parkway, Markham, Ontario L3R 4T8

Printed in the United States of America on acid free paper.

Created and produced in association with Blackbirch Graphics, Inc.
*Series Editor:* Tanya Lee Stone

### Library of Congress Cataloging-in-Publication Data

Chandler, Gary.
    Protecting our air, land, and water / by Gary Chandler and Kevin
Graham. — 1st ed.
        p.     cm. — (Making a better world)
    Includes bibliographical references and index.
    Summary: Presents examples of successful efforts to protect natural
resources and includes the names and addresses of organizations that are
involved in these endeavors.
    ISBN 0-8050-4624-0
    1. Environmental protection—Juvenile literature. [1. Environmental
protection.] I. Graham, Kevin. II. Title. III. Series: Making a better
world (New York, N.Y.)
TD170.15.C43   1996
363.7—dc20
                                        96-22659
                                          CIP
                                          AC

# Table of Contents

# Welcome to Making a Better World

Protecting our air, land, and water resources is extremely important. These natural resources not only need protecting to secure the very existence of many different plant and animal species, but they can also affect human health if they become too polluted.

In ancient times, air, water, and land resources were not in danger of being polluted or depleted. With a lot fewer people on Earth, there was plenty of undeveloped land, clean air, and sparkling water to support all of the planet's plants and animals. In addition, many cultures paid particular attention to caring for the Earth's resources. The Industrial Revolution, however, altered the way that societies had functioned for centuries and set in place a pattern for human society that still exists today.

The Industrial Revolution began in Europe in the 1700s and spread to North America in the early 1800s. Before that time, most people had lived off the land as farmers or performed labor by hand to earn a living—making shoes or clothing, for example. With the development of power-driven machines, however, workers needed to leave their homes or workshops and gather together to operate the machinery. The concept of the factory developed as a way to house these workers and the machines that they used to manufacture various products. People flocked to the cities to work in factories. In doing so, they created an urban—or city-based—civilization that greatly changed previously undeveloped land.

As factory production swelled, air pollution resulted from burning fuel. Pollutants such as chemicals and acids harmed water and land resources. The Industrial Revolution gradually evolved into today's modern society, and the world's population increased. Pollution problems became common and troublesome. Around the world, progress and expansion have taken their toll on our natural resources. In the 1960s, that toll began to be noticed by people around the world.

Gradually, the number of people concerned about protecting and preserving the environment and its resources began to grow. Today, there are groups all over the world that have created inventive ways and products to protect our planet.

All of the books in *Making a Better World* report on people—kids, parents, schools, neighborhoods, and companies—who have decided to get involved in a cause they believe in. Through their dedication, commitment, and dreams, they helped to make ours a better world. Each one of the stories in this book will lead you through the steps of what it took for some ordinary people to achieve something extraordinary. Of course, in the space of one book, we can share only a fraction of the wonderful stories that exist. After a long and complicated selection process, we have chosen what we believe are the most exciting subjects to tell you about.

We hope this book will encourage you to learn more about the protection of our natural resources. Better yet, we hope all the books in this series inspire you to get involved. There are plenty of ways that each individual—including you—can make a better world. You will find some opportunities throughout this book—and there are many others out there waiting for you to discover. If you would like to write to us for more information, the address is Earth News, P.O. Box 101413, Denver, CO, 80250.

Sincerely,

Gary Chandler
and
Kevin Graham

# CHAPTER ONE

# Clean Water for Everyone

Water is essential to our existence. The planet Earth is two thirds water and all life on Earth depends on it. But water from the oceans can only be used for a limited number of things without being desalinized (having the salt taken out). And increasingly, water is in short supply as the ever-expanding human population uses more and more of it. New ways to tap this resource are always useful.

Fortunately, water wizards and water protectors are tackling the challenge of creating and maintaining a resource of water large enough to sustain life indefinitely.

# *Ozone Eliminates Need for Chemicals*

Ozone is nature's own sanitizer. We are most familiar with the role that our atmosphere's ozone layer plays as protector against the Sun's harmful ultraviolet rays. But now, ozone is being used to eliminate the use of chlorine in swimming pools, drinking-water systems, and water supplies at zoos and aquariums.

Chlorine is a valuable disinfectant in certain cases. However, it can irritate the skin of swimmers and can be harmful to plants and animals if it is released into rivers and streams.

"The world has been using chlorine for a long time, but now there is a technology that is much more attractive and better for our environment," says Dan Katz, president of Oxygen Technologies of Lenexa, Kansas. "With less chlorine being used, less ends up in public waterways. It's just a better way to treat water."

In the atmosphere, ozone is made by lightning—by a reaction involving oxygen and electricity. Through technology, humans can produce it in much the same way. In a process called corona discharge, oxygen is passed through a device that holds electrically charged metal plates. The resulting ozone gas has three oxygen molecules, and the third atom is eager to break away. "We call it a 'hungry' atom because it will attack and destroy contaminants," Katz says. "Then the ozone quickly reverts to pure oxygen. You can't get more nonpolluting than that."

How does this happen? The hungry atom of oxygen attaches itself to contaminants in the water. This chemical action kills bacteria and viruses on contact and allows them to be collected by a pool's filtering system. The other two atoms of oxygen simply end up being part of the air we breathe.

7

Lab tests have shown ozone to be 3,000 times more effective at killing bacteria and viruses than chlorine. In small swimming pools, a water purifying system using ozone—costing roughly $1,500—drastically cuts the need for chemicals and electricity. In larger pools, some chlorine is still necessary, but the amount is typically cut by 70 to 97 percent. The owners save both energy and money.

"Once you've swam in an 'ozonated' pool, you'll never want to swim in a chlorinated pool again," Katz notes. "There's no smell or taste to the water, and no irritations to the eyes and skin. You feel like you're swimming in bottled water."

Ozone systems are used in more than 2,000 public swimming pools in Europe. Nearly all the pools in Germany now use ozone. Also, a third of Germany's more than 300 zoos and marine parks now use ozone systems. Some American zoos also use ozone. A freshwater dolphin at the Pittsburgh Zoo is thriving in an ozonated environment after suffering from the effects of chlorine.

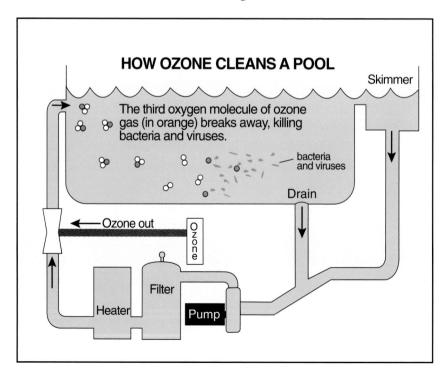

**HOW OZONE CLEANS A POOL**

Skimmer

The third oxygen molecule of ozone gas (in orange) breaks away, killing bacteria and viruses.

bacteria and viruses

Drain

Ozone out

Ozone

Heater

Filter

Pump

*New York's Central Park Zoo uses an Oxygen Technologies ozone system to purify the water for the polar bears and marine mammals.*

Oxygen Technologies is also developing a portable ozone system that could be used to purify drinking water in the developing world, which includes the poorer nations. The 14-foot-long, trailer-mounted unit would be parked near a river and could supply between 50,000 and 100,000 gallons of pure drinking water a day. The unit could run on electricity supplied by a diesel generator and would cost about $35,000.

Other uses for ozone systems include wastewater (sewage) treatment facilities used by cities, aquaculture (the raising of fish or seafood for food), and air purification. Los Angeles recently completed a $120 million drinking-water, ozone-purification facility. "People thought we were crazy at first," Katz says. "But the technology is now affordable and is getting more popular because of the efficient ozone-generating equipment being developed."

## For More Information

*Write to Oxygen Technologies, Inc., 8229 Melrose Drive, Lenexa, KS 66214, or call (913) 894-2828.*

# Waving Goodbye to High Water Costs

Americans waste an estimated 900 billion gallons of water every year. By using low-water-flow devices, recycling and re-using water, and taking other simple water-saving steps, homes and businesses could save substantial amounts of water.

The Water Alliances for Voluntary Efficiency (WAVE) program, which is run by the U.S. Environmental Protection Agency (EPA), encourages businesses to save money while saving water. "A business that is a WAVE participant is asked to look at its water use and make profitable changes," says John Flowers, program director. The program protects the environment by reducing water use, wastewater discharges, and energy use.

Reducing water consumption means that less energy is needed to heat, pump, and process water. By taking the various water-saving measures suggested by the program—such as installing special showerheads, toilets, kitchen equipment, and faucets—WAVE members can save up to 30 percent of their water and sewer costs.

WAVE's initial target has been the hotel and motel industry. Westin, Hyatt, ITT Sheraton, Outrigger, and the Saunders Hotel Group are some of the program's members. Among them, they represent nearly 600 U.S. hotel properties and more than 200,000 guest rooms. Together, WAVE members are expecting to save more than 2.25 billion gallons of water

## Hotel Efficiency Measures

| Measure | Project Cost | Savings |
|---|---|---|
| Toilet Valves | $ 5,000 | $ 2,600 |
| Showerheads | $ 5,300 | $ 14,900 |
| Cooling Tower Blowdown Control | $ 8,500 | $ 4,500 |
| Laundry Rinse Recycle | $ 28,000 | $ 8,000 |
| Ice Machine Coolant Loop | $ 8,000 | $ 20,000 |
| | $ 59,000 | $ 50,000 |

11 Million Gallons per Year
47%
14 Mo. Simple Payback

PEQUOD ASSOCIATES, INC.

per year for an annual savings of nearly $8.5 million in water, sewer, and energy costs. Water-conservation steps have been designed for every aspect of the hotels' operations, including bars, kitchens, laundry, guest rooms, cooling towers, outdoor irrigation, and landscaping.

Groups that participate in WAVE receive a computer software program called WAVE-Saver. This program helps managers and engineers keep track of water use and cost. The software also helps them identify water-saving opportunities. "Where profitable, members are asked to install [new equipment in their buildings] within an agreed-upon time frame that reduces consumption," Flowers says. "We also ask members to design their new facilities to be water-efficient and to report their progress to us."

WAVE also gives the hotels materials to share with their guests that explain how the program conserves water. People who stay at these properties learn that they are part of the

*This simple chart shows how much water and money a WAVE hotel was able to save in a year.*

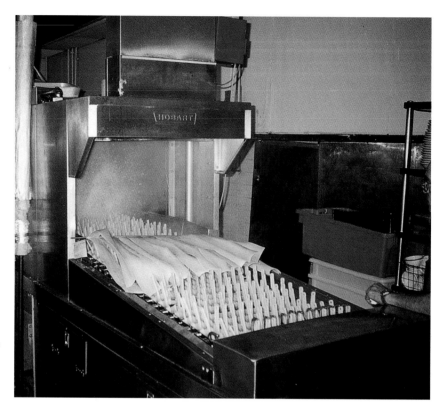

*This industrial dishwasher for glassware has been designed to conserve more water than traditional equipment.*

solution to the water problem. WAVE also staffs a nationwide help line and provides technical support and training in water conservation. WAVE estimates that if every hotel and motel participates, the combined savings would total $85 million and 32 billion gallons of water per year.

"Our next step is to expand the program to include other commercial businesses," Flowers says. "But everyone should start participating in water conservation now."

### For More Information

*Write to the WAVE Program Coordinator, U.S. EPA, 401 M Street SW, Mail Stop 4204, Washington, D.C. 20460, or call (202) 260-7288.*

# Pyramid Power Produces Fresh Water

It's hard to imagine a pile of rocks providing a steady source of fresh water, but an ancient technology—dating back many centuries—is being researched by a group of Seattle engineers for its water-production potential in modern times.

José Vilá, a civil engineer who heads the group, first came across the "pyramid phenomenon" while studying road-buckling problems in America's Southwest. Asphalt roads built in this dry region were actually falling apart due to water damage. Vilá found that the crushed rocks used as a base layer in the asphalt roads were gathering water moisture from the air. When the condensed water then dripped into, and expanded, the clay soils beneath the crushed-rock base, the roads buckled. This is called hydrogenesis (creating water). Certain combinations of air temperatures and humidity make this problem commonplace in arid regions. In wet regions that don't experience these climate conditions, hydrogenesis does not occur.

The process of hydrogenesis seemed to hold potential as a source of fresh water. To that end, Vilá and two partners started a company called Hydrogenesis Inc., in Mill Creek, Washington. Eventually, they hope to build conical pyramids of loosely piled rock—aerial wells—to capture large amounts of water vapor from the air and produce fresh water. Hydrogenesis's efforts are the first aimed at producing water on a large scale.

It is believed that ancient Crimeans first had the idea of using water condensation created by the daily heating and cooling of the air to collect water. About a century ago, at the

13

site of an ancient Crimean city, an amazing water-supply system was discovered. Thirteen pyramids, each about 40 feet tall and made of loose rocks, were connected by a series of stoneware pipes. Scientists estimated that the system probably produced almost 200,000 gallons of water a day.

In some societies today, people pile rocks around the bases of trees to gather moisture. And desert mice are known to make small piles of rocks to produce drinking water.

Although many aspects of hydrogenesis remain to be studied, Vilá believes that 40-foot-tall pyramids built of 4-inch-diameter porous rocks—such as chunks of old cinder blocks—could produce 500 gallons a day per pyramid.

"These pyramids would be inexpensive to build, require little equipment and effort, and be harmless to the environment," Vilá says. "They could be a very valuable source of water in areas where there is little inherent moisture. And no power or pumps or maintenance are required. They run on solar energy, so air pollution and waste products are not a concern."

Vilá thinks that the wells will work best in regions with big temperature changes between day and night. Water production will vary with the temperatures from season to season. A pyramid's inner portions will stay cool long into spring and summer, causing increased condensation when warm air passes over and through the cool rocks. Water would then drip down to a concrete basin and into a drain for collection.

Hydrogenesis, Inc. was awarded a National Science Foundation grant to conduct their initial research. A computer program has been developed that allows Hydrogenesis, Inc. to predict aerial-well water yields throughout the year at any location and climate. The company is now looking for funding to build a prototype (model) pyramid and measure the amounts of water actually produced.

## For More Information

*Write to Hydrogenesis, Inc., 14814 18th Court SE, Mill Creek, WA 98012, or call (206) 337-3606.*

# Wetlands Serve as Nature's Kidneys

Producing greater supplies of fresh water is not the only water-related dilemma faced by modern society. There is also the problem of what to do with wastewater—water that has been used to serve various human needs.

In Horry County, South Carolina, a sewage disposal system is currently discharging 650,000 gallons of wastewater a day into a unique wetland system. By using the wetlands—which we might call "nature's kidneys"—as water filters, the county is able to process the wastewater in an energy-efficient manner. The wetlands remain relatively unchanged. The various plants and natural systems at work in wetlands are able to clean water by removing the waste materials and using them as nutrients. This not only preserves a wetland area, but provides a community service as well.

"Fifty percent of Horry County is wetlands, so it became a natural alternative to consider," says Larry Schwartz, an environmental planner with the Grand Strand Water and Sewer Authority. The Authority handles wastewater treatment for the county. "We're just using the natural filtering ability of the land to renovate wastewater."

The wastewater is distributed across three Carolina bays, which are egg-shaped natural depressions unique to coastal regions of the Southeast. (By the way, the bays are one of the only places that Venus's-flytraps—the famous meat-eating plant—can be found in the United States.) Filled with peat and shrubs, the bays act as buffers, or filters, between the uplands and the region's fragile blackwater rivers, which are dark in color and slow-moving.

Only one bay at a time receives the wastewater. With all three bays used alternately, up to 2.5 million gallons of wastewater a day could eventually be treated as the county grows over the next 20 years. Boardwalks crisscross the bays to support pipes carrying the wastewater. Two-inch holes, spaced every 15 to 20 feet, allow the water to splash from the pipes onto rocks and disperse evenly across the bay.

The wastewater has been treated to "secondary" levels before it enters the bays, meaning that 85 percent of all the wastes, such as toilet paper, have been removed. Using humanmade treatment systems, large amounts of energy are required to finish cleaning the remaining 15 percent. "But in this case we're using energy from the Sun, which in essence

*The only Venus's-flytraps in the United States grow in the wetlands of Horry County.*

powers the wetlands," Schwartz says. "That's the beauty of it. The system is cost-effective and energy-efficient."

Many government agencies at both state and national levels are involved in the project. Two biologists work full time testing the quality of the water leaving the bays and studying the wetlands environment to make sure that the natural communities in the bays are not being harmed in any way.

The project has generated plenty of interest from other states. Some plan to construct their own wetlands for similar purposes. Wetlands can be built by copying the natural form of the ecosystem. Layers of gravel and sand are topped with a certain type of soil that supports common wetland plants such as reeds and cattails.

Schwartz gives at least one tour of the county's wastewater system a month. "It's a new way to do things," he says. "If wetlands are selected and managed properly, there is no reason not to use them."

*Wastewater is discharged through these pipes along a boardwalk system.*

## For More Information

*Write to the Grand Strand Water and Sewer Authority, P.O. Box 1537, Conway, SC 29526, or call (803) 347-4641, ext. 295.*

*17*

# America's Rivers: Crucial to Drinking-Water Supplies

America's rivers are the veins and arteries that bring life to the land. One nonprofit group with more than 15,000 members is working to protect and restore the country's river systems. Appropriately named American Rivers, the group has preserved 20,000 miles of rivers and 5 million acres of riverside land since its founding in 1973.

"We are the principal river-conservation organization in North America," says Randy Showstack, the group's director of communications. "We work on many issues, including preserving wild and scenic rivers, restoring urban rivers, and protecting endangered aquatic species." The organization's efforts include promoting public education, talking with representatives of government and industry, and supporting river-saving groups.

American Rivers is dedicated to educating the public about the importance of rivers to society. "Without healthy and clean rivers, we would have much less fresh water available for fish and wildlife or human use," Showstack explains. Flowing rivers connect the mountains to the sea and nourish the various ecosystems they pass through along the way. They serve as corridors for migratory birds and fish, as well as homes for many other plants and animals. Major threats to rivers include dam-building; overdraining for agriculture; loss of riverside habitat to development; and run-off pollution from pesticides, fertilizers, road salt, and numerous other forms of waste.

Rivers are being damaged at an alarming rate due to the increasing effects of human development. Already, 34 percent

of North America's fish species are classified as rare to extinct, along with 65 percent of its crayfishes.

Of the nation's 3.5 million miles of rivers, 600,000 miles—or about 17 percent—already have been dammed by more than 68,000 projects.

In 1995, American Rivers played a role in a success story in California. An irrigation district that had planned to construct a 400-foot-high dam on the Clavey River near Yosemite National Park was persuaded to withdraw its plans. The district realized that its water needs were not great enough to justify building the huge dam. The Clavey had been on American Rivers's annual list of the ten most-endangered North American rivers. The list aims at informing the public about the numerous and ongoing threats to various rivers and streams.

Another river in the West, the Clarks Fork of the Yellowstone River, has also attracted the attention of American Rivers. The group is fighting a proposed gold mine, partly owned by Canadian companies, which would be located near the river in Montana, about 2 miles from Yellowstone National Park. The huge mine would produce 5.5 million tons of acid waste, so a 90-foot-high dam would be needed to create a storage reservoir. Such waste from mining operations throughout the United States has already damaged more than 12,000 miles of

*19*

*American Rivers is fighting a proposed gold mine that would damage the Clarks Fork of the Yellowstone River.*

American rivers. This proposed mine presents a risk to one of America's most popular parks, its rivers, and the surrounding region.

American Rivers is also working to increase the size of the National Wild and Scenic Rivers System, established by Congress in 1968. The system preserves portions of outstanding rivers and now includes more than 150 sections of rivers that cover about 10,700 miles. But this represents less than one-third of 1 percent of the nation's river miles.

Only 19 states have studied their own rivers to learn which are in need of saving from development. "We're trying to alert the public and decision makers that our rivers—so valuable to public health, ecosystem protection, and recreational use—are not in good shape," Showstack says. "There is an urgent need to restore and protect them. We think that North America's rivers should be dealt a much kinder hand."

## For More Information

*Write to American Rivers, 1025 Vermont Avenue NW, Suite 720, Washington, D.C. 20005, or call (202) 547-6900, or visit the web site at http://www.amrivers.org/amrivers/*

# Making Air Safe to Breathe

*A*ir, like water, is essential to life. Polluted air can cause or lead to numerous health problems in humans. It can also harm plants and animals and the ecosystems in which they live.

Keeping the air clean, however, is not always easy. The most common form of air pollution is the dark haze in the air called smog. This visible pollution is caused by industry, automobiles, wood burning, and other sources. Controlling these sources of air pollution has proven difficult, because everyone likes to purchase the products that industry produces.

In addition, there are invisible forms of air pollution that could spell big trouble for the Earth in the future. These include the threat to the planet's ozone layer and the greenhouse effect. In this chapter, we discuss a number of air-related problems as well as possible remedies for them.

# *From Laundromats*
# *to Ecomats*

A company in New York is turning clean clothes into "green" clothes by keeping the environment in mind in every aspect of the laundry business. Called Ecomats, these laundries provide an alternative to dry cleaning. The Ecomats eliminate the use of perchlorethylene, called perc—a toxic (poisonous) chemical used in the standard dry-cleaning process. Perc is a petroleum-based chemical that was classified as hazardous by the EPA in the 1989 Clean Air Act.

Before creating Ecomat, Diane Weiser, president of the company, was managing apartment buildings. In 1991, when one of the properties didn't have washing machines and dryers, she decided to open a laundromat in the building. She then realized how many chemicals are used in the laundry business and decided to offer alternatives. Weiser soon learned that the EPA was studying alternatives to perc and she joined the effort. She then heard of the Ecocleaning process. An idea developed in England 50 years ago, Ecocleaning is a wet cleaning method that uses heat, steam, and natural soaps. "It involves a series of techniques that vary from garment to garment, and is the same price as dry cleaning, if not cheaper," says Weiser. "In many cases, wet cleaning provides better quality than perc, because perc is basically a degreaser and doesn't deal well with water-based stains like sweat."

Perc has been blamed for polluting the air and ground water. It has also been blamed for health problems in residents

of apartment buildings where dry cleaners operate on the ground floor.

Ecomats also feature water-conserving washing machines and energy-efficient dryers. And the only soaps for sale in an Ecomat are all-natural and biodegradable, meaning that they will decay naturally without harming the environment. Even Ecomat's delivery van is environmentally friendly: It runs on natural gas instead of gasoline.

"We're helping make people aware of the issue of using perc," Weiser says. "We address the issues by giving people a cost-effective alternative that not only prevents perc from being released into the air and water, but also gives people an alternative for cleaner clothing. We're helping protect the environment by showing that you don't need to use a toxic chemical."

*An Ecomat technician launders a garment in this system that eliminates the need for perc and conserves water and energy.*

## For More Information

*Write to Ecomat, 147 Palmer Avenue, Mamaroneck, NY 10543, or call (914) 777-3600.*

## Creating a Super-Refrigerator

In a corporate effort aimed at protecting the atmosphere, a new super-efficient, chlorofluorocarbon (CFC)-free refrigerator, built by the Whirlpool Corporation, has won a "golden carrot" award in an industry competition sponsored by 24 utility companies nationwide. To win the $30 million prize in this Super Efficient Refrigerator Program (SERP), Whirlpool competed with several other appliance manufacturers that had also developed super-efficient refrigerators.

Whirlpool's winning design uses 25 to 50 percent less energy than 1993 federal standards required. Unlike previous models, the refrigerator accomplishes this without the use of the ozone-destroying CFCs. In addition, computer technology allows the appliance to defrost only when necessary. The first SERP model hit the market in 1994. The refrigerator/freezers are available under the Whirlpool, KitchenAid, and Kenmore brands.

Whirlpool also developed one of the first devices to help automotive and appliance repairers capture CFCs when fixing older cooling units. The airtight bags are designed to hold the CFCs from several refrigerators or automobiles until the CFCs can be extracted for recycling.

"The progression in environmental benefits in our appliances has been great during the last five years," says T. R. Reed, Whirlpool's manager of financial communications. "Apart from the money savings, the energy-efficiency and CFC-free features make a big difference in the environment. And consumers don't have to give anything up."

The idea for the contest began in 1989, when representatives from the Natural Resources Defense Council (NRDC), a number of utility companies, and the EPA met to explore ways to reduce energy consumption. The representatives knew that refrigerator makers were redesigning their products to meet new EPA guidelines banning CFCs and requiring more energy efficiency. The utility companies wanted to promote energy savings. Refrigerators consume as much as 20 percent of a home's electricity, so they wanted to see refrigerator makers go beyond the new EPA requirements.

Before long, the SERP competition came to life in the form of a nonprofit corporation funded by a group of public and private utility companies. The goal was to bring more environmentally friendly refrigerator/freezers to consumers before they would normally reach stores. The award money that Whirlpool won will be used to cover extraordinary design, development, and marketing costs—as well as more expensive materials and parts—so that consumers will find SERP refrigerator prices similar to those of other models.

Whirlpool expects to manufacture roughly 250,000 SERP refrigerators in a variety of models by the end of 1997, when the program ends. "The real winners in this competition are the American consumers who purchase SERP products," Reed says. "They will benefit from the advanced technology, and know they've helped to protect the environment. Ultimately, it's their purchasing decisions that will determine the success of the SERP program."

## For More Information
*Write to SERP, 3050 K Street, Suite 400, Washington, D.C. 20007, or call (800) 927-3985.*

# Preserving the Land

What land belongs in the hands of private owners, and what land should remain open to the public for all to enjoy? There are no easy answers to these questions.

Land is one of our most important natural resources. It provides society with food and shelter as well as with settings that help keep people in touch with the natural world. It also provides for the very existence of the plant and animal worlds. The problem is that often, once land is changed from its original state through any number of forms of development, it can never be returned to that state.

For example, when a redwood forest is felled (cut down) for timber production, centuries worth of growth disappears and the land takes on an entirely different character. Pro-development forces say that the lumber gained is worth the altered state of the land left in logging's wake. The environmental community and other groups, on the other hand, argue that enough forests have already been destroyed—some should remain intact. This chapter discusses various issues involving land and describes efforts under way to protect and conserve portions of this great resource.

# Indian Tribes Work to Protect Ancient Lands

**A** "wilderness council" composed of 11 Native American tribes has been working since 1986 to create America's first intertribal park along California's northern coast. The 3,900-acre tract of land, located in Mendocino County, once held dense fir forests, tranquil oak meadows, and towering stands of fog-shrouded redwood trees. And long ago, the land supported the largest concentration of Native Americans in North America. The Sinkyone people (pronounced "sin-kee-own") inhabited this land for 10,000 years, until the mid-1800s. Then, for 30 harsh years, settlers and the U.S. military massacred many of the Sinkyone and chased the remainder off their land so that logging activities could be undertaken. Some Sinkyone children were even sold into slavery.

A century later, modern logging operations finished taking most of the redwood trees on the land and destroyed the lush rainforest. Only 2 percent of the area's original old-growth forest remains standing today. "Now we are faced with degraded watersheds and ecosystems because of over-logging," says Hawk Rosales, executive director of the InterTribal Sinkyone Wilderness Council. "Much of the land is devastated from clear-cutting and subsequent erosion. Since 1986, we have been bringing our communities together and have been using both native and modern approaches to restore the land."

A mid-1980s lawsuit stopped the Georgia-Pacific logging company's plans to clear-cut the Sally Bell Grove, which the

*This photograph shows the effects of clearcut logging on Sinkyone land.*

California Department of Forestry had approved for harvesting. The 90-acre grove of old-growth redwoods is named after one of the Sinkyone massacre survivors who watched as her parents were slaughtered by white vigilantes. In July 1985, a California appeals court ruled that the Department of Forestry had violated the state's environmental laws.

In 1986, a total of 7,100 Sinkyone acres were purchased from Georgia-Pacific. Nearly half of the land was added to the Sinkyone Wilderness State Park.

The remaining 3,900 acres, called the Sinkyone Upland Parcel, was purchased by the Trust for Public Land through a $1.1 million loan from the California State Coastal Conservancy (a state agency). The Conservancy then agreed to come up with a plan for reselling the 3,900 acres to a local public interest organization. The timber industry had hoped that those 3,900 acres would again be made available for commercial logging uses. But the Wilderness Council set its sights on using the land as a place for creating a unique park in memorial to its Native American ancestors.

In 1995, the Coastal Conservancy Board sided with the InterTribal Sinkyone Wilderness Council, agreeing to sell the land to the group for $1.4 million. "Our goal was always to acquire the land. Now we have a chance to restore it to its original balance through Native American uses and stewardship," says Rosales.

The Council is now leading efforts to restore the land. By bringing together university researchers and other professionals with Native American community members, various projects are combining traditional land-management methods with modern approaches. Plans are under way to remove logging roads and restore parts of the land. They are also restoring some of the streams that once teemed with salmon. Other projects include maintaining a nursery for native trees and shrubs, planting redwood seedlings, and removing brush.

Preserving Sinkyone cultural resources is a major focus of the Council. "Sinkyone contains important cultural resources considered sacred by Native American people of this area," Rosales says. "Local native people are still strongly connected to this land, which they use for ceremonial and food-gathering purposes. We want the park to be the living model of Native American land stewardship that Indian people practiced here for thousands of years."

*Bear Harbor, in northern Sinkyone territory, is one of the beautiful wilderness areas being preserved.*

*An intertribal group of Pomo and Wailaki people dance together at a Sinkyone cultural gathering.*

Eventually, the Council hopes to open the park to the public and manage it with local Native Americans. The area contains many sacred archaeological sites that remain culturally significant to the descendants of the Sinkyone people and would be of interest to all visitors. In addition, four small village sites will be incorporated into the park—all built with traditional materials in traditional ways. The sites will be used for retreats, cultural activities, and ceremonies.

A documentary, *The Run to Save Sinkyone*, has been produced by the Wilderness Council about the fight to save the land and future plans for the park. Three years in the making, the film won an award in 1995 at Robert Redford's Sundance Film Festival.

### For More Information

*Write to the InterTribal Sinkyone Wilderness Council, 190 Ford Road, #333, Ukiah, CA 95482, or call (707) 463-6745.*

## Trust Preserves Land for Future Generations

Some land conservation organizations are very broad in reach. One, the Trust for Public Land (TPL), works to protect national land for people—be it expansive wilderness or a city lot set aside for a park or public garden. Formed in 1973, this nonprofit organization operates 17 offices around the United States and has completed more than 1,000 projects, protecting nearly 1 million acres of land in 43 states.

"The Trust for Public Land is a conservation, real-estate organization," says TPL's president, Martin Rosen. "We work in the marketplace on transactions that result in land for public use and many times help solve complex problems associated with land protection. Basically, we see that the public is represented at the negotiating table."

TPL frequently works with community groups and government agencies to acquire land threatened by development. It is the only national conservation group specifically established to conserve land for public use and open space. When there is public support to protect land as a park, TPL is able to secure the land. TPL then works with government agencies or nonprofit conservation organizations.

Some projects involve preserving river corridors and forests while allowing adjoining lands to be used for development such as housing. In Grand Junction, Colorado, for example, an unsightly junkyard beside the Colorado River was transformed into a riverfront "greenbelt," which is an area of woods, parks, or open land in a community.

TPL protects land in both rural and metropolitan settings, but much of its work is accomplished in city neighborhoods that do not have enough parks and open space for people to use. In New York City, for instance, an asphalt traffic triangle was reborn as a park. TPL's Green Cities Initiative targets 12 large U.S. cities, where the Trust believes opportunities, leadership, and community commitment will lend support to land acquisition and park-improvement programs. The five-year project includes the metropolitan areas of Boston, Seattle,

*TPL preserved the land for Senka Park in Illinois to be enjoyed by all.*

Atlanta, Cleveland, Baltimore, New York, Los Angeles, and San Francisco, among others. The initiative aims at increasing public awareness concerning the vital role parks and open space play in the quality of urban life.

"We see our unique role as connecting land with people—and it is in urban areas that most of America's people live," Rosen says. "Having a natural place to go is important to people. We see this effort as a way to bring more people into the environmental movement. A city lot full of vegetables and flowers offers a touch of nature for residents that can mean more to them than a piece of land a hundred times larger in a remote setting. And because the projects typically are accomplished through community involvement, they can help instill in the population a respect and sense of responsibility for the environment."

*At a TPL site that was once an abandoned section of a city block, a community garden thrives.*

## For More Information

*Write to the Trust for Public Land, 116 New Montgomery Street, Fourth Floor, San Francisco, CA 94105, or call (800) 714-LAND.*

# Transforming Rails to Trails

Another unique land-acquisition group draws its resources from America's great heritage in railroads. In the late 1800s, the United States started building a huge, interconnected system of railroad lines. By 1916, that system had become the largest in the world, with more than 250,000 miles of track. But as transportation methods changed, thousands of miles of these railroad tracks began falling out of use. Today, more than 3,000 miles of track are abandoned each year. A total of 160,000 miles have already been abandoned.

In an effort to conserve these corridors for public use, Rails-to-Trails Conservancy is working to convert these abandoned railroad lines into multi-use trails. Founded in 1986, the nonprofit group has already celebrated the opening of the 500th rail-trail—an 11-mile stretch in Massachusetts called the Minuteman Trail, which runs through the historic town of Lexington and follows part of the route that Paul Revere rode in April 1776. Today, America's rail-trail network has passed the 7,000-mile mark.

Rail-trails can be found in 48 states, with Michigan leading the way with 87 trails. Another 1,100 projects are under way across the country that will add more than 12,000 miles of trails.

The trails provide plenty of recreation on very little land. A mere 200 acres of unused rail corridor can provide a park and trail more than 20 miles long. Rail-trails are flat and well-graded. Thus, they are appropriate for a number of uses, from bicycling and walking to horseback riding and cross-country skiing. The trails are not open to cars, providing a much-needed open space for people of all ages and abilities.

Creating rail-trails became viable after Congress passed the 1983 National Trails Act, which preserves railroad corridors intact for future transportation use, while allowing them to be used in the meantime as trails. "Our goal is to convert as many of these abandoned railroad corridors into trails as possible and create an interconnected network of trails throughout the country," says Steve Emmett-Mattox, the group's community-affairs coordinator. "Some day people will be able to travel from coast to coast on these trails."

*Rails-to-trails workers replace old railroad tracks and revitalize the land with trails that can be used by everyone.*

*Rails-to-Trails projects have preserved some of the last open areas of land in some regions of the country.*

Much like the Trust for Public Land, Rails-to-Trails Conservancy acts as a resource, helping various volunteer groups, private foundations, and park agencies to create new trails. The Conservancy assists these local groups in following proper legal procedures and seeing the sometimes-lengthy process through to completion.

"Once created, rail-trails can serve both recreational users and daily commuters—linking homes, businesses, and parks. They provide useful routes away from the world of motorized vehicles," Emmett-Mattox says. "Many times, these trails are the last section of open land in urban areas. They are a swath of green space and a refreshing escape from congested areas."

### For More Information
*Write to Rails-to-Trails Conservancy, 1400 16th Street NW, Suite 300, Washington, D.C. 20036, or call (202) 797-5400.*

## Vacations that Educate and Preserve

**H**ave you ever wanted to track a wolf, dig up a dinosaur, help a hatchling sea turtle run to the sea, save a rhino, or figure out how monkey society works? For most of us, nature and adventure programs on public television are about as close as we ever get to actually going on a scientific research expedition. Besides watching from the sidelines, however, there's another option that allows you to work—often in remote places—with scientists tackling some of Earth's most intriguing and troublesome problems.

For more than two decades, Earthwatch has proven that nonscientists can make important contributions to scientific field research. Earthwatch has been sending out teams of volunteers, who invest their time and energy in the future of the planet while they experience the uniqueness of different cultures and ecosystems. Since 1972, Earthwatch has mobilized more than 40,000 people to join its EarthCorps. These people pay their own way and work—typically for two weeks—assisting leading scientists and scholars in researching critical environmental issues.

Projects range from saving endangered black rhinos in Zimbabwe, to creating management plans for Brazil's threatened rainforests, to studying the effects of tourism on a U.S. national park. Specific Earthwatch successes include saving thousands of endangered sea-turtle hatchlings on the Caribbean island of

St. Croix, discovering new species of rainforest-canopy insects in Peru, and documenting Native American rock art in Utah. The organization's projects are listed in *Earthwatch* magazine, which is sent to the more than 35,000 members of Earthwatch six times a year.

One project under way in Kenya has Earthwatch volunteers working with local communities to build ovens powered by solar energy. Millions of people in the poorer nations of the world such as Kenya rely on wood and other traditional fuels for more than 50 percent of their energy. Cutting and burning wood contributes to a number of environmental problems, such as deforestation and health problems, including respiratory illnesses. Solar power and other renewable energy sources seem like obvious solutions to these problems, but they have been used only rarely and have not been sufficiently tested in these areas.

*As a female leatherback nests on St. Croix, an Earthwatch team carefully records the number of eggs laid, as well as the time, weather, and flipper tag number.*

"Our projects provide a wonderful way to accomplish a number of different objectives. Apart from assisting scientists who need the volunteer talent to help them do their work, we also do a lot of training of teachers and young people from the host countries," says Brian Rosborough, chairman of Earthwatch. "By assigning native people to different expeditions, they can bring back knowledge and understanding to share with their own communities in the countries where we are working."

*This is one of about 300 solar ovens built by Earthwatch volunteers and local communities in Kenya.*

## For More Information

*Write to Earthwatch, Box 403BV, Watertown, MA 02272, or call (800) 776-0188.*

# Trees: Taking Care of the World's Lungs

*F*orests and the billions of trees that compose them are considered the "lungs of the world." This is because they convert carbon dioxide into oxygen, which humans and other creatures need in order to live. Forests also provide vital habitats for thousands of plant and animal species.

There are several types of forests on Earth. The planet's rainforests exist primarily in hot, moist regions near the equator. Temperate forests exist in areas of the Earth where cooler temperatures usually prevail. In addition, forests can be composed of primarily coniferous (evergreen) trees, such as pine and fir trees, or hardwood trees, such as maples and oaks, or a mixture of the two types.

Unfortunately, the world's forests continue to be felled due to society's numerous demands, a process called deforestation. Half of the world's population depends on wood for basic needs such as cooking, light, and heat. In addition, just one quarter of the world's population consumes fully three quarters of all processed paper and board. This consumption is one of the leading causes of deforestation.

## Saving Ancient Forests

The logging of the world's endangered rainforests receives a great deal of notice and publicity. Deforestation of old-growth forests located in the temperate regions of the Earth do not get as much attention, but they also need protection from logging and other practices.

Old-growth forests are composed of many ancient trees that can be hundreds of years old. These old trees are desirable to loggers because their size and width can provide plenty of lumber. New-growth forests are composed primarily of smaller, younger trees.

Fortunately, a California nonprofit group is heading up the effort to save critical old-growth habitat. Called Ancient Forests International (AFI), the group is recording the distribution of these vanishing ecological treasures and promoting their preservation.

The nonprofit organization began after its director, Rick Klein, worked as a park ranger in Chile. He kept hearing rumors of trees similar to redwoods, called alerce cypress, that grew in the South American country's southern regions. However, all he could ever find were stumps of the trees. After returning to the United States, Klein met loggers who had cut down alerce trees in Chile while working for U.S. logging companies.

He then organized a group of people interested in finding some of the trees still standing. In 1989, they traveled to Chile and hiked high into numerous valleys in search of the alerce trees. These rare trees can live more than 3,000 years, a life span second only to bristlecone pine trees. Eventually, the group found a number of the huge trees in large tracts of cool and damp ancient forests.

Since then, AFI has helped raise the issues of forest use and preservation in Chile, and placed the legendary forests on Chile's national political agenda. The group also helped form Chile's first non-governmental organization focused specifically on old-growth issues. Through this group, AFI has helped in efforts to buy more than 500,000 acres of ancient forest in Chile. AFI itself purchased land for Chile's first private park—a 1,200-acre piece of forest in the country's famed Lake District. Called the Cañi Forest Sanctuary, the park is dedicated primarily to environmental education efforts.

In addition, AFI is working on projects involving temperate forests in New Zealand, Tasmania, the Pacific Northwest,

*With AFI's help, more than 500,000 acres of forested land in Chile have been preserved.*

Poland, and Russia. Russia contains 20 percent of the world's forests; in Siberia alone, 30 percent of the world's old-growth forests remain standing. However, this area is under increased pressure by international companies like South Korea's Hyundai Corporation, which is clear-cutting on the Syetlaya Peninsula and threatening the existence of the endangered Siberian tiger. The old-growth forests are being pulped for newspapers and toilet paper rolls in the United States, Europe, and Japan.

"Temperate forests epitomize the cool, dark, cathedral-like essence of old-growth ecosystems, and the race is on to save the last of these ancient forests," says AFI member Kathy Glass. "They're all being cut, and anything we can do to spread awareness and create action is important. We feel very passionately about the issue."

Ancient Forests International runs an action and information center in the heart of redwood country in northern California. It works to conduct its own innovative environmental education activities, and it also networks to help other organizations in various efforts to save old-growth forests.

*Araucaria trees in the Cañi Forest Sanctuary are being protected by AFI.*

## For More Information

*Write to Ancient Forests International, P.O. Box 1850, Redway, CA 95560, or call (707) 923-3015.*

# California Lumber Receives Seal of Approval

**A**nother California-based forestry group has been working to create a "good-forest-keeping seal of approval" through a system aimed at identifying lumber from forests in the western part of the United States that is harvested in a way that doesn't harm the forest or the land. The Institute for Sustainable Forestry (ISF) calls for land owners and logging operations to follow ten elements of sustainability in harvesting their forests. These elements aim at sustaining—or keeping alive—the forest for future generations to use and enjoy.

To receive a seal of approval, the forests cannot be clear-cut (entirely cut down), doused with harmful chemicals to kill certain types of vegetation, or torn up by an abundance of roads built for logging operations. Protecting all the various plants and animals in the forest, along with enhancing local employment opportunities, are also important criteria. "ISF does not aim to stop logging," says Jude Wait, executive director of the ISF. "What we need is a more ecologically sound and sustainable way to do it. ISF is bridging the gap between environmental concerns and economic realities."

The idea for sustainable logging grew out of a company called Wild Iris Forestry in Redway, California. Owners Peggy and the late Jan Iris cut down only a small number of the hardwoods on their land and sold the kiln-dried wood for flooring and cabinets. The Institute is taking the forestry system developed at Wild Iris and passing it on. "You can't have economic stability without ecological stability," Wait says. "So in a lot of ways, this is a community-development project, as well as an environmental effort." In other words, if there were not enough jobs to support the population, the forests would be clear-cut to provide a living for the people of the area.

The ISF labeling program, called Pacific Certified Ecological Forest Products (PCEFP), first requires land owners or logging operators to develop a timber-management plan. This plan provides an inventory of what trees are on the land, lays out long-term goals for the land, and describes how the ten elements of sustainability will be met.

The elements include the following practices and efforts:

- Forest practices will maintain and/or restore the beauty, vitality, and functioning of the natural processes of the forest ecosystem and its components.
- Forest practices will maintain and/or restore surface and groundwater quality and quantity.
- Forest practices will maintain and/or restore the natural process of soil fertility, productivity, and stability.
- Forest practices will maintain and/or restore a natural balance and diversity of native species of the area for purposes of the long-term health of ecosystems.
- Forest practices will encourage a natural regeneration of the native plant species.
- Forest practices will not include the use of artificial chemical fertilizers or synthetic chemical pesticides.
- Forest practitioners will address the need for local employment and community stability and will respect workers' rights.
- Sites of archaeological, cultural, and historic significance will be protected and will receive special consideration.
- Forest practices will be of the appropriate size, scale, time frame, and technology for the parcel of land, and will adopt an appropriate monitoring program.
- Ancient forests will not undergo any commercial logging while the Institute participates in research on the impact of management in these areas.

*45*

*The ISF holds workshops to teach land owners and loggers how to implement the ten elements of sustainability.*

When tree harvesting is started, periodic inspections are undertaken by the Institute, along with the normal inspections conducted by the state government. If all conditions are met, the eventual lumber produced will carry the PCEFP label.

By purchasing the certified and labeled wood, consumers know that their buying power is supporting sustainable forestry and allowing them to influence forest-management policies. Lumber companies, in turn, have a marketing advantage through the creation of a special market, much like that enjoyed by organic food producers. The Institute works together with wood-product businesses, government agencies, university researchers, and economic-development and forest-advocacy groups.

"Working together makes a sustainable, ecologically based forest product industry more feasible and takes some pressure off the remaining old-growth forests," Wait says.

## For More Information

*Write to the Institute for Sustainable Forestry, P.O. Box 1580, Redway, CA 95560, or call (707) 923-4719.*

# Planting Pieces of History

founded in 1875, the American Forests organization is itself part of America's history. It is the country's oldest nonprofit citizens' organization for conservation efforts. American Forests has a unique tree-planting program to put a piece of America's history in anyone's yard. The Famous & Historic Tree Program combines contemporary conservation with America's heritage. Young trees that are direct descendants of trees planted by, or associated with, George Washington, Betsy Ross, Martin Luther King, Jr., and 130 other famous people and places are available for planting through this program.

"We've identified trees all across America and around the world that are associated with significant people or events in history," says Jeff Meyer, project director of American Forests. "From the seeds of those one-of-a-kind trees, we grow small, healthy trees and make them available for sale."

An estimated 100 million tree-planting spaces are now

*Alex Haley's nephew, David, helps school kids plant an Alex Haley Silver Maple in the author's honor.*

available around homes and businesses in U.S. towns and cities. Planting those trees could save as much as $4 billion each year in energy costs by blocking the Sun and cutting air-conditioning costs, and by blocking cold winter winds and saving on heating bills. Those energy savings would reduce carbon dioxide emissions from energy production by an estimated 18 million tons per year.

Included in the program catalog are descendants of trees that predate the landing of Christopher Columbus, the American Revolution, and the bloody battles of the Civil War. Others were nurtured by presidents, inventors, artists, heroes, and other accomplished Americans. George Washington, for instance, planted numerous trees at his home in Mount Vernon, Virginia. The program's George Washington tulip poplar dates back to 1785 and is the largest of the living trees planted by the first president.

Other small, direct-offspring trees have been grown from seeds hand-picked from the trees of Abraham Lincoln, Ulysses S. Grant, Robert E. Lee, John James Audubon, Edgar Allen Poe, Helen Keller, Jesse Owens, Thomas Edison, and Henry Ford. Some of the most popular selections come from Walden Woods in Concord, Massachusetts. Because this is where Henry David Thoreau lived and wrote from 1845 to 1847, it is a sacred tract of land to many. Recording artist Don Henley and other celebrities founded the Walden Woods Project, aimed at stopping development on the land through fund-raising and public-awareness activities.

In addition, the nation held many events to remember Franklin Delano Roosevelt in 1995. American Forests marked the 50th anniversary of the death of President Roosevelt by offering six species of trees in his honor. The trees were descendants of Roosevelt's trees. The group introduced a white oak from Hyde Park, New York, and a redbud, or southern magnolia, from Warm Springs, Georgia. "As governor of New York during the Great Depression, Roosevelt arranged for thousands of unemployed people to work on reforestation

The Walden Woods Project was founded by Don Henley (front row, left) and other celebrities dedicated to preserving forests. Shown planting a Walden Woods Red Maple tree with schoolchildren and Don Henley are Jon Lovitz, Queen Latifah, Lou Diamond Phillips, Jennifer Tilly, Dana Delaney, Jeff Bridges, Bette Midler, Elizabeth Peña, Luther Vandross, Bonnie Raitt, and Ed Begley, Jr.

projects," Meyer says. "Therefore, these trees seemed an appropriate symbol for FDR."

In addition to its Famous & Historic Tree Program, the group manages several other programs in which kids can get involved. These include Global ReLeaf and the *National Register of Big Trees*.

In an American Forests program, kids in Washington, D.C., planted trees with senators and members of Congress.

Global ReLeaf is an effort aimed at restoring damaged forests across the United States by planting trees to provide wildlife habitats and protect streams and rivers. Nearly 3 million trees have been planted since Global ReLeaf began in 1990. Hundreds of thousands of people have helped by planting 64 Global ReLeaf forests in 32 states, and more efforts are planned.

The *National Register of Big Trees* encourages tree lovers to search for, identify, and help preserve the biggest tree of each species in the United States. The biggest reported trees are listed in the *Register*, which is published every other year. It was last published in 1996.

This education-and-action program decides on the more than 800 champion and co-champion trees by combining measurements of their heights, their trunk circumferences, and the spread of their branches. Some tree species still don't have champions, meaning that you could find one of the country's oldest trees and get it registered.

## For More Information

*Write to American Forests, P.O. Box 2000, Washington, D.C. 20013, or call (800) 320-TREE. You can also call (800) 8-ReLeaf.*

# Building Political Power for the Environment

**P**olitics plays a huge role in providing protection for our air, land, and water resources—or allowing them to be sacrificed and polluted in the name of "progress." Political actions taken over the years in Washington, D.C., as well as in every state, have provided many safeguards for our air, water, and land. However, there is no guarantee that these safeguards will remain in place.

You can help by supporting various organizations that can make your voice heard by the nation's politicians. You can also write directly to your politicians to let them know how you feel about various environmental issues. This chapter describes several organizations that work to see that our air, land, and water resources are protected by the government.

# Electing an Environmentally Aware Congress

There are plenty of environmental groups working to help the Earth through various political avenues. But only one—the League of Conservation Voters (LCV)—works exclusively to elect candidates that support conservation causes to the U.S. Congress. The League's mission is simple: Get a majority of candidates who support environmental protection elected to the U.S. Senate and House of Representatives and hold those elected accountable for their environmental voting records in Congress.

"LCV is the bipartisan political arm of the U.S. environmental movement. That's what we've been since 1970, when leaders of the environmental movement decided that they needed to try and influence Congress," says Deb Callahan, the League's president. "We use the tools of political campaigns to elect pro-environment candidates to Congress who will vote for the environment."

To that end, each year LCV produces a *National Environmental Scorecard*, which scores all members of Congress on their support of (or lack of support for) environmental protection. The Scorecard is sent to the League's more than 60,000 individual members and the media. It includes information on the most important environmental issues voted on in Congress and details the environmental voting records for each legislator, state delegation, and region of the country.

The issues considered on each Scorecard reflect the consensus of the U.S. environmental movement. Experts from 27 mainstream conservation organizations meet and decide which votes in Congress are most crucial to the nation's environment. A score ranging from 0 to 100 percent—with 100 being the best—is then registered for each member of Congress.

The Scorecard summing up the work of the first session of the 104th U.S. Congress, for example, considered votes on such issues as clean water, endangered species protection, and national parks and wilderness. Unfortunately, the environmental scores in Congress were at an all-time low in 1995. The national average for the Senate was at 47 percent; the House's national average was 43 percent. Providing the public with timely information on how their representatives vote to safeguard their health is more important now than ever.

In order to satisfy special-interest demands, Callahan explains that politicians often vote to eliminate or minimize conservation protections for the air we breathe, the water we drink, and the land on which we raise our families. To counteract this, LCV educates the public by supporting pro-environment candidates and highlighting environmental issues in races involving strong anti-environment candidates.

*Former secretary of the interior Stewart Udall discusses the need for environmental leadership with the League of Conservation Voters.*

## For More Information

*Write to the League of Conservation Voters, 1707 L Street NW, Suite 750, Washington, D.C. 20036, or call (202) 785-8683.*

# Working to Save Utah's Wild Lands

**F**ar from Washington's Capitol Hill, a Utah nonprofit group is concentrating on a narrower political realm but working just as hard to protect an ecosystem that is dear to the hearts of thousands of people. Through a combination of research, public education, legislation, and litigation, the Southern Utah Wilderness Alliance (SUWA) is dedicated to making sure that the red-rock wilderness of this western state is protected.

Formed in the early 1980s, the group's main goal revolves around a proposal to protect 5.7 million acres of southern Utah public land as part of the National Wilderness Preservation System. The public lands surrounding Utah's spectacular national parks are characterized by equally impressive arches, buttes, canyons, pinnacles, and large expanses of slickrock—all composed of varying shades of brilliant orange and red sandstone.

To fight for more wilderness, SUWA has joined with more than 100 other organizations to form the Utah Wilderness Coalition. The proposal pursued by the Coalition would protect numerous archaeological sites, pristine canyon systems, and critical wildlife habitat and migratory routes from development. Their proposal would protect as wilderness 5.7 of the 22 million acres of Bureau of Land Management (BLM) land in Utah.

The proposal has been sponsored in the U.S. House of Representatives by Representative Maurice Hinchey of New York State and co-sponsored by more than 110 other representatives.

However, a competing proposal introduced by Utah's congressional delegation in 1995 would designate significantly less land as wilderness. What is more, it would not allow Congress to ever designate the land as wilderness again.

"We're in the midst of a public-education campaign to broaden support nationally for the citizens' wilderness proposal," says SUWA executive director Mike Matz. "Because these are federal public lands, we are trying to reach out to people across the country who know the wonders of Utah's red-rock country and create a national effort. Unless we succeed, what remains of Utah's spectacular wild lands will be handed over to various industries. America's red-rock wilderness deserves better. SUWA protects public lands in Utah for the types of values that are often ignored. We are advocates for recreation, wildlife, and healthy ecosystems."

All SUWA members receive a quarterly magazine updating them on progress and setbacks on many fronts concerning Utah's canyon country. The publication also gives members opportunities to get involved by encouraging letter-writing and phone-call campaigns aimed at various politicians.

*SUWA is working to protect the Dirty Devil River and its canyons.*

*Factory Butte in Utah is another threatened area being designated as "wilderness" in SUWA's proposal.*

Numerous short articles update readers about news on the area's national forests, well-known canyons, government agencies, and industry development plans.

Profiles of SUWA's board of directors are also featured. New Mexico's Jim Baca is the latest addition to the group's board. Baca served as the director of the Bureau of Land Management in the Clinton administration until he ran into political trouble because of his push for real reform of public land policies, including grazing and mining programs.

"As far as wilderness is concerned, there is no more important environmental fight than the fight for southern Utah," Baca says in the SUWA publication. "I believe in organizations like SUWA and their ability to garner real grassroots support. Without grassroots involvement, we cannot expect to win battles, and southern Utah is going to be wasted."

## For More Information

*Write to the Southern Utah Wilderness Alliance, 1471 South 1100 East, Salt Lake City, UT 84105-2423, or call (801) 486-3161*

# Working to Save Forests

In 1988, while hiking in Wyoming's Medicine Bow National Forest, Leila Stanfield, Don Duerr, and Jeff Kessler came across tract after tract of land once forested, which had been clear-cut. "It looked like a war zone," Stanfield says. "We got upset and decided to try and figure out why it was happening. We had to determine what the U.S. Forest Service did and how the government system of timber sales worked. To learn more, we went on field trips with the Forest Service and Fish and Game and began to study forest ecology."

That process led to the formation of a local environmental group initially called Friends of the Bow, which focused on preserving what remained of the Medicine Bow forest. Later, in a battle that landed on the pages of a number of the state's newspapers, several representatives of Wyoming industry groups involved in livestock, farming, trucking, and mining incorporated the "Friends of the Bow" name, taking it away from its originators. Today, while still using the name Friends of the Bow on an informal basis, the Laramie-based environmental effort operates as a nonprofit group incorporated as Biodiversity Associates.

Initially, the group started requesting maps and information about proposed timber sales from the U.S. Forest Service. In addition, Stanfield, a private pilot, and Duerr and Kessler, both photographers, began flying over the forest to monitor logging operations. "By 1990, we had a shocking array of photos and had discovered through Forest Service documents that the Medicine Bow was the most heavily logged and road-riddled forest in the southern Rocky Mountains," Stanfield says. "We started doing slide shows to raise awareness about the extent of clear-cutting and its impacts."

Clear-cutting fragments the natural forest, removing rich nutrients and displacing certain wildlife species. It can lead to the extinction of various species of plants and animals—or the loss of biodiversity—as well as serious soil-erosion problems.

The aerial photography effort also revealed six main roadless, non-cut areas remaining in the forest. The group set out to save these remaining parcels of forest because the Forest Service at the time planned to log all six. By getting local citizens involved, the group persuaded the Forest Service to institute a logging ban in the six roadless areas. The ban may remain in place, though, only until a new forest plan is developed later in this decade.

"Our concern is that the Forest Service looks only at the number of trees cut, not at all the problems caused by clear-cutting—many that are harmful to a number of wildlife

*Leila Stanfield surveys a clear-cut area of Wyoming's Medicine Bow National Forest.*

species," Stanfield says. "The Forest Service is supposed to protect these species. We want proof that the remaining pieces of forest are sufficient to ensure these species are safe."

Today, the group immerses itself in a great deal of technical work as it tries to work with the Forest Service on master plans being developed for national forests in Colorado, Wyoming, and South Dakota. Master plans for many of these states' national forests will be created by the turn of the century. "In the past, we've challenged timber sales scheduled ten years ago in the old forest plan. One by one, the Forest Service put out the project documents, and we appealed them and filed lawsuits to try and stop them. Now we're trying to work with the Forest Service while these plans are in the development phase," Stanfield says. "We are jumping in at the beginning of the process to try and create long-term, positive change."

*Leila Stanfield sits on top of a wasteful "slash pile." These piles are made from trees that logging companies cut down but don't use because of size.*

## For More Information

*Write to Biodiversity Associates/Friends of the Bow, P.O. Box 6032, Laramie, WY 82070, or call (307) 742-7978.*

# Letter Writing Can Make a Difference

Who says that writing letters to politicians can't make a difference for the environment? Politicians read their mail and can be affected by what they read. Writing a letter is a great way to affect all kinds of political decisions.

Many people realize how important protecting the environment is to their very existence and are working to ensure that the Earth remains in good shape in the future. They are writing letters to their politicians and telling them how they feel.

The letters you send to your local, state, and national representatives really can make a difference. And it's easy. For example, you could write a general letter saying that you want forests in your state to be protected and pollution to be stopped. Or, when you learn about a specific issue that concerns you, you can write to your politicians and tell them what you think should be done to address the problem.

Call your local newspaper or look in the telephone book to get the names and addresses of the politicians that represent you and your family as well as your neighborhood, city, and state. To write your representative and senators in Washington, D.C., simply get their names and address your letters to:

Sen. _____
United States Senate
Washington, D.C. 20510

Rep. _____
U.S. House of Representatives
Washington, D.C. 20515

# Glossary

**advocacy**  support of an idea or a policy

**aerial**  of, in, or produced by air

**aggregate**  Various loose materials such as sand, gravel, or pebbles.

**aquaculture**  The cultivation of aquatic plants and animals, such as fish and seaweed, for human consumption.

**arid**  extremely dry

**biodiversity**  The combined diversity of plant and animal species on Earth.

**bipartisan**  of, relating to, or involving members of two parties; usually refers to Democrat and Republican parties

**chlorofluorocarbons** (CFCs)  Chemicals used as refrigerants that damage the atmospheric ozone layer.

**clear-cut**  To cut down all of the trees in a section of forest.

**climatic**  pertaining to climate

**condensation**  The process of turning a gas or vapor into a liquid.

**contaminant**  Something that diminishes the purity of a substance; a pollutant.

**deforestation**  to clear of forests or trees

**greenhouse effect**  The phenomenon of atmospheric heating in which carbon dioxide and other gases act like glass in a greenhouse by trapping more and more of the Sun's heat, causing increasing warming on Earth.

**habitat**  The natural environment of an organism.

**hydrology**  A science dealing with the properties, distribution, and circulation of water.

**inhospitable**  lacking favorable conditions

**ozone gas**  A form of oxygen produced when an electric spark is passed through air.

**ozone layer**  The layer of the upper atmosphere where most atmospheric ozone is concentrated.

**porous**  able to be passed through by liquid or air

**pristine**  pure and undisturbed

**respiration**  The process by which organisms take in oxygen.

**sanitizer**  A substance for killing bacteria.

**slickrock**  A sandstone rock formation that is smooth and slippery, found abundantly in Utah and other parts of the American Southwest.

**stewardship**  Managing and taking care of any number of things, including the environment.

**temperate**  moderate in temperature

**toxic**  having the effect of a poison

# Further Reading

Cossi, Olga. *Water Wars: The Fight to Control and Conserve Nature's Most Precious Resource*. Morristown, NJ: Silver Burdett, 1993.

DeStefano, Susan. *Chico Mendes: Fight for the Forest*. New York: Twenty-First Century, 1992.

Dolan, Edward F. *The American Wilderness and Its Future: Conservation Versus Use*. Danbury, CT: Watts, 1992.

Goldstein, Natalie. *Rebuilding Prairies and Forests*. Danbury, CT: Children's Press, 1994.

Lucas, Eileen. *Naturalists, Conservationists, and Environmentalists*. New York: Facts On File, 1994.

———. *Water: A Resource in Crisis*. Danbury, CT: Children's Press, 1991.

Whitman, Sylvia. *This Land Is Your Land: The American Conservation Movement*. Minneapolis, MN: Lerner, 1994.

# Index

## Photo Credits

Cover: C. P. S./P. McCloskey; page 9: Courtesy Central Park Zoo/Oxygen Technologies, Inc.; pages 11, 12: Pequod Associates, Inc.; page 16: ©Howard Miller/Photo Researchers, Inc.; page 17: Grand Strand Water & Sewer Authority; page 19: ©Victor McMahan/American Rivers; page 20: ©Margaret Bowman/American Rivers; page 23: Photos by Laine W. Wilder/Ecomat; pages 28, 29, 30: Courtesy InterTribal Sinkyone Wilderness Council; pages 32, 33: ©Ken Sherman; pages 35, 36: Rails-to-Trails Conservancy; page 38: ©Russ Schleipman; page 39: ©Daniel Kammen; pages 42, 43: ©Stephen Millard; page 46: Institute for Sustainable Forestry; pages 47, 49, 50: American Forests; page 53: Fischer Photography; pages 55, 56: ©1995 James W. Kay; pages 58, 59: Biodiversity Associates/Friends of the Bow.

Graphics by Blackbirch Graphics, Inc.